Passion
of the
Heart

Gary M Pratt

authorHOUSE®

AuthorHouse™
1663 Liberty Drive
Bloomington, IN 47403
www.authorhouse.com
Phone: 1 (800) 839-8640

Published by AuthorHouse 05/12/2017

ISBN: 978-1-5246-9173-8 (sc)
ISBN: 978-1-5246-9172-1 (e)

Table of Contents

Allow My Heart

I travel upon the open road,
I seek my destiny,
Behind walls I do not like,
Is this the life for me,
Where do I go from here my friend,
Allow my heart to see.

The din of urban streets is loud,
It grows throughout the years,
And yet it seems that no one cares,
Must we supress our fears,
Where do I go from here my friend,
Allow my heart to hear.

I seek forgiveness from within,
My soul you cannot steal,
Is what I want from life so bad,
Can my needs be real,
Where do I go from here my friend,
Allow my heart to feel.

True are feelings from the heart,
Yours I wish to see,
Is it so bad to show your love,
To someone just like me,
Do we go on from here my friend,
Allow my heart to bleed.

All That They Are Worth

Help me through my troubled life,
I wish only to bfree,
I'm trapped within this empty shell,
For all eternity,
My hopes and dreams forever lost,
Yes, that is how I feel,
Trapped within this empty shell.
Like an ever-spinning wheel.

I seek only happiness,
For all the children of this earth,
To us, they give their hearts and souls,
All that they are worth,
I want to see their innocent smiles,
Written upon their face,
To build for them a happy home,
Within this human race.
'
I can conquer mountains high,
Mighty rivers I can cross,
Forever seeking hope and joy,
I never judge the cost,
Of freedom for my fellow man,
Their will come a time,
For peace and love and harmony,
I'll never look behind.

Don't put me on a pedestal,
A martyr I'll ever be,
I only wish to be a part,
Of this democracy,
To give back part of what I take,
From this troubled land,
Give to me your love within,
Reach out and take my hand.

An Angel With Silver Wings

He only has one wish in life,
To soar the heavens high,
The loneliness he does not feel,
No pleasure undenied,
For this is where he wants to be,
A man with silver wings,
To soar through clouds of milky white.
To hear the Angels sing.

A pilot is a pilots friend,
Or so that's how it seems,
I know of no one else in life,
Who live beyond their dreams,
A leasure undenied to those,
Who's feet must hug the earth,
His passion lives beyond my reach,
For all that he is worth.

I loved him like no other could,
His passing undenied,
If ever I should miss him,
hen my eyes shall search the sky,
A ilot soaring high in life,
He did pot get to be,
Yet fly he will forevermore,
An Angel with silver wings.

And So My Heart Can Rest

Silently,
I stare upon,
Creation at its best,
The seed of life,
Was planted here,
And nature did the rest.

Her fingers seem,
So small to me,
And yet, her grip is strong,
My celebration,
Is her life,
And this cannot be wrong.

Within my heart,
The missing link,
Was love for one who cared,
And in return,
Was ecstasy,
That caught me unawares.

For no one here,
Could ever replace,
What I see in your eyes,
A love returned, Unconditionally,
Is one that never dies.

So silently,
I stare upon,
Creation at its best,
My daughter, you are,
Everything to me,
And so my heart can rest.

And So My Heart Is Free

The choices that we make in life,
Are sometimes full of strife,
And so we gain the strength to choose,
What we want from life.

My love for you was strong enough,
To satisfy a need,
To give my heart and soul to you,
And then to watch them bleed.

I only asked for in return,
What you could never show,
A feeling shown from deep within,
That you will never know.

I tried to find a reason why,
You tore my world apart,
You never even tried to see,
The beauty of my heart.

But I am strong enough to know,
That I will always be,
What you could never see inside,
And so my heart is free.

An Everlasting Light

When youthful souls,
Perchance to meet,
And kiss each others hearts,
A life is built,
Around their love,
And that is just the start.

And in each passing,
Year there grows,
An everlasting light,
That glows within,
Two hearts alike,
And shines so very bright.

And when our time,
Has come to pass,
And we must say goodbye,
Our hearts will live,
In memories,
Reflected in your eyes.

You both shall always,
Be as one,
Your souls shall never part,
The light that was,
The one you loved,
Still shines within your heart.

A Question Strong

A question strong,
Within my mind,
That's always asking why,
I choose to do,
The things which hurt,
Your feelings held inside.

I broke the trust,
Within your heart,
And let my feelings stray,
And still you're always,
On my mind,
And so my soul must pay.

My loneliness,
Is never worth,
The cost of missing you,
Too long I've lived,
Without your touch,
And so my heart did lose.

I hope that time,
Can heal the scars,
I've placed upon your heart,
A single wish,
From me to you,
Allow a brand new start.

If I can mend,
The broken bridge,
That starts our lives anew,
Can you forgive,
My broken heart,
The choice is up to you.

A Rose Upon Your Hearts

The two of you,
Have tested time,
And know that love can live,
If what you feel,
Within your hearts,
Beans more than what you give.

I've seen you waging,
Battles strong,
And always you survive,
For what you share,
Is destiny,
That cannot be denied.

And even though,
Temptation tries,
To make a true heart stray,
The heart which sees,
The path to love,
Will always lead the way.

And so I know,
That what I see,
Is love that's tried and true,
I'll place a rose,
Upon your hearts,
A gift from me to you.

A Spaceman Came A' Travelin'

A spaceman came a'travelin',
From a far and distant sun,
Not knowing what he's looking for,
Not knowing anyone,
A master of the place he's from,
A castaway on the wind,
Knowing not,
he's in a race,
That he can never win.

Small in size,
but big in heart,
He knows not what to do,
Go forward, back,
which way to go, Oh,
why must we always choose,
He knows not of the danger,
Of which he holds in his hands,
To spread the seeds of destiny,
Across these sacred lands.

Which way is up,
Which way is down,
He cares not for these things,
The only one,
He cares about,
Is the angel of his dreams,
She fills his heart,
With joy and hope,
Such things he'll never know,
Forever through, The universe,
The lonely spaceman goes.

So off to conquer worlds,
That are never there to see,
Bitter is the spaceman,
Who knows he'll never be,
A common man among us,
He feels so all alone,
To ask forever the question.

As The Songbird Cries

I don't ask for riches,
They only bring me pain,
And I don't ask for wishes,
That bring me only shame,
I don't ask for freedom,
If there's none to be found,
And I don't ask for poverty,
There's plenty all around.

Lonely is the little child,
Who has no friends to see,
And lonely is the bird of prey,
Who knows he has to feed,
Lonely are the elderly,
Abandoned from our lives,
Lonely is the night so cold,
As the songbird cries.

I love the things you say to me,
Whispers in the night,
And I love to hear children laugh,
And play with all their might,
I love cotton candy,
And sailing on the sea,
And I love you so very much,
For what you give to me.

Joyfull are the little pups,
Playing in the grass,
And joyfull is your loving smile,
Forever shall it last,
Joyfull is the little girl,
ho rides the pony free,
And joyfull is the way I feel,
For what you give to me.

Because You Are The Best

We've known each other,
For so long,
And always our love grows,
Our hearts grow stronger,
With each touch,
And in your eyes it shows.

A subtle glance,
Across the room,
Says our hearts are fine,
For both our hearts,
Are solid gold,
We've shared so much in time.

And every time,
I wake with you,
It puts my heart to rest,
For always dear,
Our love is true,
Because you are the best.

But For Now

Conquistadors,
Of legends told,
Are buried in my mind,
Ancient tales,
Of forgotten lore,
I thought I'd never find,
Memories,
I cannot share,
Seeming so unkind,
But for now my tongue I shall not seek to hold.

Darkness kills,
The light of day,
In shadows my soul shall sleep,
Quiet whispers, Upon the wind,
Into my thoughts they creep,
Gentle tears,
Forever flow,
My eyes they do not weep,
But for now my heart could never be so bold.

Love is lost,
For those who seek,
For what could never be,
Your poison flows,
From tainted fruit,
That grew upon the tree,
Yet you could spark,
My fires within.
And set my passions free,
But for now the flame is out and I am cold.

Cassandra's Rose

The petals of her skin so soft,
Is passion to the touch,
I almost lost what I never thought,
That I could miss so much.

Her whispers in my ear carress,
The senses of my soul,
If passion be a two-way street,
Then down this path I go.

How can one so small in size,
Be so big in heart,
The wrapping hid the package well,
And so we both did part.

But in her mind I could not leave,
She could not let me go,
And so her wounded heart did yearn,
For the love I did not show.

But love can conquer many wars,
Within two hearts alike,
Win it shall and win it did,
For I am hers tonight.

A fire burns within her eyes,
And everybody knows,
My love for her burns eternally,
For I'm Cassandra's Rose.

Do They Really Cry For Me

Your voice it whispers on the wind,
It does not call my name,
My heart is filled with love for you,
So why do I feel shame.

The tears that well within your eyes,
Do they flow for me,
I wish that I could touch your heart,
But would it set you free.

Your flowing locks of golden light,
Caress my skin no more,
The graceful movement of your steps,
No longer reach my door.

The night is cold and yet I pulse,
With rage I cannot hide,
I do not like this inner voice,
Yet how long must I try.

I wish that I could touch your heart,
Yet this could never be,
The tears that flow from your swollen eyes
Do they really cry for me.

Dreams

I wake before,
The light of day,
And rub my restless eyes,
These dreams that keep me,
From my sleep,
To me are no surprise.

And as the daylight,
Breaks on through,
The darkness of the night,
I sit and question,
What it is,
That causes so much fright.

The answers which,
Should be so clear,
Confuse me even more,
I wish to travel,
Beyond these walls,
But I cannot find the door.

And as the darkness,
Creeps up upon,
My heart which cannot weep,
I'll seek salvation,
In my dreams, Forever my retreat.

Eternal Is My Love

Eternal is my love for you,
Whose heart is solid gold,
The passion and the joy we share,
Never shall grow old.

When I look into your eyes,
I know my heart can rest,
For I know, above all else,
That I have found the best.

You gave my heart a place to go,
For that I'll always be,
Thankful for the love you give,
Which grows inside of me.

And so, eternal is my love,
For one whose heart is gold,
I give you all I have inside,
My love, my heart, my soul.

Forever

If I leave it all behind,
To seek what's sheltered in my mind,
Will I rejoice for what I find,
Or will my fears remain.

If I wander through the night,
To seek what some say isn't right,
Will my mind put up a fight,
Or will my soul feel pain.

If I take a chance and start,
To seek your lonely,
bleeding heart,
Will our lives push us apart,
Or love will we finally gain.

If I walk along the shore,
To seek what's gone forevermore,
Will I end up at your door,
Forever to remain.

Forever Roaming Free

Journey through the everlasting,
Tales of lust and lore,
Read through secret passages,
To find the hidden door,
If what you find is what you seek,
Then though shall not need me,
For lonely is the wanderer,
Forever roaming free.

I've been to lands so full of life,
Yet not a soul I've seen,
Confusion clouds my sheltered mind,
Whatever can it mean,
I've no desire to catch the ring,
This ride is not for me,
For I'm the lonely wanderer,
Forever roaming free.

I know you know of who I am,
You've seen my face before,
Look into the mirror,
Choose the only unlocked door,
Join me if you really dare,
Be sure of what you see,
Yes I'm the lonely wanderer,
Forever roaming free.

Heaven At My Door

Lonely is the night so cold,
When Stars refuse to shine,
Forever waiting patiently,
When black shall turn to wine,
But if the loneliness is shared,
No longer shall I pray,
To see the hours flashing past,
When night shall turn to day.

My heart can   fall so easily,
If what I feel is right,
The line is cast from deep within,
And yet I hold on tight,
To give my love so freely,
Is a cautious step indeed,
Could someone help me trust myself,
Perhaps believe in me.

The choices that we make in life,
Are chances that we take,
Question them and lose your mind,
But never love forsake.
I've made a choice that's right for me,
My mind is put to rest,
Never will my heart be cold,
To me you are the best.

So lay your head upon my heart,
And put your mind to rest,
The comfort that you offer me.
Can only be the best,
To feel your touch so soft and warm,
Is heaven at my door,
My heart can fall so easily,
Perhaps forevermore.

Hiding Down Below

In the quiet of the evening,
Solely lit by candlelight,
Shadows hide in corners,
To scare with all their might,
Children wandering aimlessly,
Down creepy, creaking stairs,
What waits in hiding down below,
They really couldn't care.

In oceans calm and peaceful,
There hides a raging storm,
Creatures lurk in darkness,
Where the waters never warm,
Divers search for what they want,
First come, first serve is fair,
What waits in hiding down below.
They really couldn't care.

In the misty rays of morning,
A rocket breaks the sky,
Destination, outward bound,
Should we question why,
Pilots flying heavy loads,
Sometimes unaware,
What waits in hiding down below,
They really couldn't care.

Hope

The depths of your persuasion,
My resistance cannot match,
Wicked is your evil plan,
Within the plot you hatch.

Boiling is the blood that flows,
Within your evil shell,
And no amount of sanity,
Will save you from your hell.

Deeper is the grave YOU dig,
And in it shall you die,
Never will you rise again,
To spread your evil lies.

Three wishes I did give to you.
You've only one wish more,
Use it wisely, think it out,
You've now erred twice before.

Now hope is all that's left for you,
Is it enough to start,
Think of those who love you most,
And wish Yourself a heart.

I Am Hers Tonight

I sit and gaze upon the soul,
That rests her weary head,
Upon the pillow of my heart,
Where lonely tears were shed.

Comfort is her only wish,
And this I shall give free,
She knows the cost is nothing more,
Than what he gives to me.

As I carress the golden locks,
That fall upon her breast,
I know that heaven I have found,
And so my heart can rest.

She wakens quietly and sighs,
And smiles when she sees,
That her and I shall be as one,
Our passions flowing free.

She knows that I am hers tonight,
And so she drifts to sleep,
Her memories are in my heart,
To cherish and to keep.

I sit and gaze upon the soul,
And know that this is right,
For I have kissed her golden heart,
And I am hers tonight.

I Am Not Alone

Her table holds a place for one,
Her bed she does net share,
She spends her days and nights alone,
I wonder if she cares.

To me she is a soul that's lost,
And yet her heart is brave,
I'm saddened by this life she lives,
For hers I cannot save.

And so I sit as hours pass,
And ask her once again,
If this is what she's looking for,
Someone to share her pain.

She sheds a tear for what she lost,
And slowly lifts her head,
It hurts to look into her eyes,
I look away instead.

And as I turn to walk away,
She whispers out my name,
I turn to see her reaching out,
And so I must remain.

She struggles with her inner voice,
It tells her to beware,
But voices aren't as strong as hearts,
When willing to be shared.

I hold within my hands the hopes,
Of innocence so pure,
Touch my soul and feel my strength,
Your heart I wish to cure.

She reaches out and finds the key,
To doors she could not pry,
She opens up her heart to me,
Her pain she cannot hide.

I see a shining ray of hope,
A rainbow in her eyes,
Her heart has touched what once was lost, And soon I realize.

If I can heal your broken heart,
And give your soul a home,
Then always will my heart be free,
For I am not alone.

If Only

The silent night is deafening,
Upon his shattered ears,
A friendly voice could make him smile,
If only he could hear.

The darkness haunts I'm evermore,
Yet he envisions more than me,
A smile could really warm his heart,
If only he could see.

The odors drifting on the breeze,
For him are such a waste,
He could enjoy what he has not,
If only he could taste.

The stench of death is in the air,
Where is the eternal well,
A drink could give him life anew,
If only he could smell.

His hands are lost to forces strong,
The loss did cost too much,
To feel her would be heaven at last,
If only he could touch.

I'll Always Give My Heart

The paths we choose,
To take in life,
Begin upon the day,
When life is sprung,
From love and joy,
That sets us on our way.

And as each passing,
Day begins,   -
We learn a little more,
From those who take,
The time to show us,
What lies beyond the door.

If we should stumble,
Trip or fall,
They always lend a hand,
And even though,
We make mistakes,
They try to understand.

And so to you,
My Mom and Dad,
I'll always give my heart,
I thank you for,
The love we share,
And for giving my life a start.

Let Your Feelings Show

People come and go but never,
Do I see their pain,
The shadows of my deadened heart,
Shall never once again,
Be open to the hurt you give,
And still I must remain.

The subtle touch of fingertips,
Upon your skin so soft,
Ignites what cannot be replaced,
And is forever lost,
The heart and mind must be as one,
And so I pay the cost.

Your eyes they tell me stories which,
I've never heard before,
Your touch it tells me only that,
I can remain no more,
And if I cannot melt your heart,
Then should I find the door.

Now I believe in fate alone,
For fate is all I know,
So tell me that your love remains,
And I will never go,
Your heart is all you left for me,
Please let your feelings show.

Listen

Listen to the raindrops,
Of tears that gently flow,
From deep within the souls of those,
Who never seem to show,
The feelings held within the heart,
That beats so soft and free,
To give a little of the mind,
Is never to costly.

The gentleness upon your face,
Is beauty from within,
These thoughts that travel through my mind,
Forever full of sin,
I cannot sacrifice my life,
To give you what you want,
I'll share with you my heart and soul,
My mind you shall not haunt.

If peaceful winds still blow across,
The gentle seas at night,
Then I shall do my best to help you,
Make it all seem right,
The laughter of the lonely cricket,
Who beckons from afar,
Is only heard on certain nights,
When our cares, we disregard.

If power brings you happiness,
And greed still sets you free,
Then loneliness shall be your friend,
For you shall not have me,
You lust for love through what you take,
From those you cannot buy,
And yet it seems that all I see,
Are tears within your eyes.

A gentle kiss upon the cheek,
Will usually tend to show,
The love between two hearts alike,
Like softly falling snow,
If passion is your only friend,
And lust is all you feel,
Then the love you give from deep within,
Must surely not be real.

If you sit and listen hard,
To what you want to hear,
Will you hear the same old lies,
You repeat every year,
Or will you listen from the body,
The heart, the mind, the soul,
The truth shall always be with you,
And you shall reach your goals.

Lonely Is The Sandman

All these hopes and dreams,
Will they last throughout the day,
Shatter all my sorrows,
To high a price to pay,
I've never been to England,
But I sure would like to go,
Why must there be a reason,
For what I'll never know.

Lonely is the sandman,
Who feels he'll never see,
The simple joys of life,
Only wanting to be free,
He wishes to be happy,
If only for awhile,
To witness all the pleasures,
Of the newborn baby child.

Look into my empty eyes,
Tell me what you see,
Is he knocking at the door,
Begging to be free,
Born to wander aimlessly,
Throughout this lonely land,
Try to stop him if you dare,
Catch me if you can.

I wish only to be free,
From these earthly binds,
If I took the time to try,
I know I'd leave behind,
Happiness and joy for all,
The children of this earth,
Lonely is the sandman,
Who feels he has no worth.

My Heart Awaits

Brittle are the shards of glass,
Falling from your eyes,
Ask me any questions dared,
But tell my thoughts no lies,
My feelings have no secrets left,
And so my heart must die.

Painful are my fingertips,
When touching you so soft,
The senseless voices in the night,
Shall send my soul aloft,
I'll listen to your whispered words,
No matter what the cost.

Heavy are your footsteps which,
Remind me of my past,
Dare to crawl through secret doors,
To find if love can last,
My heart awaits to pay its toll,
And so the die is cast.

My Heart I'll Share

You know that I would kiss your heart,
If you could set it free,
Your love and trust are buried deep,
Beneath the pain I see.

The doors of which you've passed before,
For you, were only lies,
I know your heart holds many scars,
Reflections in your eyes.

I only wish to give you that,
Which should belong to you,
The trust of one who needs your love,
And one who's heart is true.

Allow my love to flow within,
And mend your broken heart,
Let your emotions touch my soul,
And never shall they part.

I wish that you could kiss my heart,
I know that you do care,
Allow yourself another chance,
With you, my heart I'll share.

My Heart Is Blessed

Every day,
I sit and think,
And try to understand,
The reasons for,
My purpose here,
Upon this sacred land.

Until I met,
A shining star,
With fire in her eyes,
Whose heart can give,
As much as mine,
And never question why.

Her beauty,
Radiates a glow,
That sets my soul afire,
Her passion pulses,
Through her veins,
And fills me with desire.

Now she is all,
The world to me,
For I have found the best,
Her love is my strength,
Forevermore,
And so my heart is blessed.

My Heart Is Mine

You and I,
Once shared a dream,
That only couples do,
What I held,
Within my heart,
I sacrificed for you.

And when a dream,
Has lost it's charm,
There's nothing left to say,
I tried to tell you,
The reasons why,
My heart has turned away.

The time has long since,
Passed me by,
To get on with my life,
Because you will not,
Let my heart go,
My feelings for you die.

If you refuse,
To let me go,
Then I shall have no choice,
But to show you,
My life is mine,
And you will know my voice.

My Heart Still Seeks A Home

Through passages of time I walk,
And yet it never seems,
That any closer do I get,
To long-forgotten dreams.

I thought I found the peace of mind,
To see me through my day,
I thought that love was at my door,
But heaven walked away.

My inner thoughts, they only seek,
To keep me all alone,
The wait is much too long for me,
My heart still seeks a home.

If what you need is happiness,
I'll set your passions free,
Could you unlock your bolted heart,
Reach out and take the key.

I haven't much to offer yet,
But what I have is true,
So if your hand can turn the key,
Then my heart I give to you.

My Memories Decieve

I cannot quench,
The everlasting,
Thirst within your eyes,
Memories,
Decieve me,
Doth my heart dare tell me lies.

The lust you feel,
Within thyself,
Shall only serve to decieve,
My beating heart,
It feels no love,
For me, their is no reprieve.

Aimlessly,
I wander through,
My lonely days and nights,
A single soul,
I cannot find,
To make me feel all right.

Bitterness,
Will try to keep,
Me down forevermore,
Desires keep,
My soul alive,
But what am I looking for.

Confusion keeps,
My mind alert,
It holds no love for me,
Yet will I ever,
See the day,
When it shall set me free.

Your eyes,
they beckon, From afar,
The thirst is strong indeed,
I'll quench your lust,
Forevermore,
My memories decieve.

My Proudest Day

The passion and the gracefulness,
I see upon your face,
Springs to life my lonely heart,
For it has found it's place.

Within the love and joy inside,
A heart that cares so much,
I know your love for me is true,
I feel it in your touch.

The softness of your lips on mine,
Releases feelings strong,
The blood within my heart does race,
And helps me carry on.

And as Irun my fingers through,
Your sensual locks of gold,
A tingling courses through my veins, Releasing passions untold.

To touch your skin is heaven still,
And that will never die,
For you will always be my love,
My heart could never lie.

I will always be with you,
For you are all I need,
You give so much of who you are,
And that .is true indeed.

You are a lady through and through,
I'm glad you're in my life,
My proudest day is when I say,
Hello, this is my wife.

My Solitude

The simple pleasures,
Of my mind,
Satisfy my needs,
My heart could never,
Be involved,
For it would only bleed.

And so my soul,
Is sacrificed,
To feelings I deny,
And never do I,
Question that,
Which keeps me asking why.

The subtle touch,
Of whispered words,
That gently kiss my ear,
Are those I lost,
So long ago,
When once I called you dear.

My emotions,
Are restrained,
And these I cannot find,
A choice was made,
That changed my life,
But I don't really mind.

For I have found,
My solitude,
Within my sheltered soul,
And there I'll stay,
So when I die,
I'll have somewhere to go.

MY Stubborn Mind

I separate my heart and soul,
To satisfy your mind,
And yet I cannot answer why,
My reasoning is blind.

I tried to find your stubborn heart,
It seems my times a waste,
The closer I did get to you,
The harder was the chase.

The walls of which you hide behind,
Are not so very strong,
To knock them down is harder still,
And yet I struggle on.

For you are worth the time I waste,
Upon your cold, cold heart,
I'll never change my stubborn mind,
For there we'll never part.

And even though I'll lose the fight,
In the end I shall win,
For in my mind your heart shall stay, Forever trapped within.

Paradise

Paradise,
An empty dream,
Do I dare to reach,
Loneliness.
A hollow shell,
Whatever could I teach.

Children,
Give us only love,
For hate they do not know,
Myself,
I learned the lesson well,
I only hope it shows.

Animals,
They carefully watch,
The passing of the day,
Damaged,
Beyond their own control,
They do not have a say.

Forgiveness,
Is what I give to you,
But have you really learned,
Paradise,
Is in the heart,
Forever shall yours yearn.

Poverty

The rythym of the dancing lights,
That glow within your eyes,
Shall entrance those unaware,
Of how they mesmerize,
I seek the lust entraped within,
3ut do I seek a lie.

Enraptured by your trusting touch,
I did not heed the signs,
Unaware was I who could not,
Read bettween the lines,
And so I took the bait you held,
And lost my peace of mind.

Now I walk my path alone,
A victim of despair,
In alleys darkened as your heart,
which has no love to share,
Poverty you are my friend,
My friend is everywhere.

Reflections Of My Childhood

Reflections of my childhood,
Remind me of a time,
When life was simply nothing more,
Than what would cost a dime.

As I think back on paths I've worn,
Through jungles thick and deep,
I wonder if I touched your heart,
Or only made it weep.

To live within my hopes and dreams,
Is not an easy task,
A little help along the way,
Is not to much to ask.

And every now and then I fall,
And all that I can do,
Is get back on my feet again,
Let each step follow through.

Reflections of my childhood,
Remind me of a day,
When love was unconditional,
For all our hearts, I pray.

Scattered Tears

The Gods of Norse once sailed the skies,
On clouds of milky white,
Their golden chariots drawn by steeds,
Who run with all their might,
A mighty roar shall tremble through,
The darkness of the night,
And scattered tears shall fall upon the earth.

A gentle voice shall whisper near,
To calm the fear you show,
Be not afraid of thoughts uncertain,
But of things you already know,
Caution is the card we're dealt,
It tells us where to go,
And scattered tears still fall upon the earth.

I hear you crying all alone,
I wish to stop the pain,
Your eyes reveal what you could give,
But tell me what I gain,
My heart is all I have for you,
And within you'll remain,
Forever your scattered tears upon the earth.

Seasons

Spring is life, For all to see,
A smell is in the air,
Flowers bloom,
And can you see,
The love that's everywhere.

Summer comes,
School is out,
The children play so free,
Ponies run,
Through open fields,
To eat the grass so green.

Auttumn blows,
The winds of change,
When leaves shall turn to brown,
A chill is in,
The air tonight,
The frost is on the ground.

Winter gives us,
Winter games,
The snow is everywhere,
To ride across,
This magic land,
Is love for all to share.

Now seasons come,
And seasons go,
Return they always do,
Enjoy them all,
Forevermore,
Their here for me and you.

She Puts My Mind At Ease

I gaze upon the gentle face,
Of one so dear to me,
So peacefully sleeping in my arms,
She puts my mind at ease.

I could give her everything,
But mine,
it's not to give,
I can only try my best,
For in my heart she'll live.

She sighs and wakens in the night,
And stares into my eyes,
I do not know of what she thinks,
Her heart would never lie.

Her touch upon my skin is soft,
It always makes me feel,
That love is life forevermore,
To me it's oh so real.

I softly whisper in her ear,
She gives her heart to me,
I kiss her cheek so soft and warm,
As she drifts off to sleep.

She Waits Forevermore

Quietly, she sits and waits,
A word she does not say,
Forever waiting patiently,
There is no other way.

A whispered voice upon the wind,
Gently kisses her ears,
She feels the passion flowing from,
The pearls of her tears.

Her face is oh so beautiful,
This is not how she feels,
The love she thinks she's looking for,
To her is never real.

Confusion sets her mind to race,
Oh how long must she wait,
A chill goes racing up her spine,
Is St. Peter at the gate.

She could not find her happiness,
Alone upon this earth,
How long must she search for love,
Does the cost outweigh the worth.

Patience is her only friend,
Her happiness denied,
And so she waits forevermore,
As she stares down at the sky.

Shying From The Day

The ghostman sails on clouds of white,
through rays of misty coloured light,
Praying only for the night,
Whilst shying from the day.

Creatures lurk in shadows deep,
Into our lives they slowly creep, Our freedom lost and so we weep,
Still shying from the day.

If love is just beyond the door,
And the game is played without a score,
Then search I will forevermore,
Always shying from the day.

That's How It Should Be

Darkness clouds my vision,
I only wish to see,
What it is that makes me think,
We don't get much for free.

I've often felt that life is never,
Fair to those who try,
To make the best of everything,
Forever asking why.

Nighttime brings me freedom,
From things I do not hate,
Questioning my thoughts within,
Only makes me wait.

I wish to travel through my mind,
Gain access to my dreams,
Float on clouds of misty white,
Or so, that's how it seems.

My friend you are forevermore,
That's all I'll ever need,
I like you just the way you are,
And that's how it should be.

The Battle Within

Mortal man,
Can masquerade,
The silence of his heart,
Even if,
The thundering,
Tears his soul apart.

Boiling blood,
That's stirred by rage,
Sends sanity astray,
A war upon,
A battlefield,
Where deadly games are played.

Watery eyes,
Which cannot pierce,
The night which never ends,
Long forgotten,
Are the dreams,
Of ordinary men.

Silent thoughts,
Are memories,
Never to be set free,
It seems this life,
Was chosen by,
Someone other than me.

This cannot be,
My destiny,
For I am so much more,
I cannot cry,
For what I've lost,
Within this lousy war.

I gaze upon,
A lonely grave,
But no name do I see,
I wonder if,
This empty hole,
Is all that's left for me.

This war shall never,
End unless,
My heart and soul are one,
And so my battle,
Rages on,
Until my day is done.

For only sleep,
Can bring a peace,
Which no one should forsake,
I wish to rest,
Eternally,
Never to awake.

The Fascination Wins

She sits and watches,
Angels fly,
Through trees on silken wings,
The wonderous awe,
Upon her face,
Speaks of many things.

So beautiful are,
The sights and sounds,
And yet, she doesn't care,
She'll sit and watch,
So faithfully,
Sometimes unaware.

Of what the story,
Tries to say,
The message held within,
To her it's just,
An awesome tale,
The fascination wins.

She tries to keep,
Her mind alert,
The show is oh so long,
The end is far,
So far away,
To miss it would be wrong.

The beauty of,
The forest,
Is a treasure that begins,
With love for every,
Creature there,
To lose it is a sin.

But of these things,
She doesn't care,
The beauty of the show is in,
What she sees through,
Her own eyes,
And so, the fascination wins.

The Life

As a child, I wander,
Alone in life,
I wonder,
If ever I should ponder,
Is anyone there for me.

As a teen,
I worry,
Why adults,
Always hurry,
I've often felt the fury,
That boils within me.

As a parent,
I see,
hat lie has done,
For me,
as it worth the wait to see,
That life's not all it seems.

As an elder,
I wonder,
Too much I tried,
To w ander,
Do I have the time to ponder,
Is there more for me.

The Mirror

I see destruction,
In your eyes,
For what,
I do not know,
Your heart shall yearn,
Forevermore,
For what it cannot show.

The evil pulsing,
Through your veins,
Is not for me to see,
And everything,
You'll never feel,
Is what I wish to be.

And through your wrinkled,
Pores shall seep,
The hatred that you ooze,
The velvet skin of,
Life shall weep,
For what it cannot lose.

And so I wish for,
You a heart,
But this can never be,
For I can never,
Reach into,
The mirror in front of me.

The One You Left Behind

The poisons of your lifeless soul,
Reflected in your eyes,
The darkness traps the light within,
And no one questions why.

The nature of the beast is strong,
When hearts no longer care,
The things that make you run and hide,
Have trapped you unawares.

The voice that whispers in the night,
And softly tickles your ear,
Is loudest when it says exactly,
What you want to hear.

You lust for things you cannot have,
Because your mind is weak,
And when you don't agree with life,
You turn the other cheek.

And when the hands of death reach forth,
One thought shall clear your mind,
The one who could have saved your soul,
Was the one you left behind.

The Pages Of Your Heart

You turn the pages,
Of your heart,
With kindness,
joy and care,
Your smile kisses,
Even those,
Whose lives have known despair.

Your gentle voice,
Whispered soft,
Shall open deafened ears,
Your charm and grace,
Will see you through,
The silence of your fears.

Your strength is in,
The beauty of,
The person who you are,
And that which gets you,
Through each day,
Shall take you very far.

I'll read the pages,
Of your heart,
And read them once again,
My heart has known,
A little more joy,
Because you are my friend.

The Search Is Finally Over

The early morning beckons,
With the gentle light of day,
I search for words I cannot find,
There isn't much to say.

My life's been empty for so long,
My destiny denied,
It's not so hard to feel my heart,
If only you would try.

The cry is strong when souls are lost, Forever they doth seek,
A gentle ear is all they ask,
A voice that will not speak.

I wish to share my life with you,
But will you give to me,
The love you cannot give yourself,
Is hatred all you see.

Listen to my beating heart,
And tell me what you hear,
Open up the secret door,
Share with me your fears.

I can give you happiness,
Just set your passions free,
Give your heart forevermore,
Yes give your life to me.

Reach your hand, don't be afraid,
I'll love you till the end,
Your search is finally over now,
You'll never search again.

The Seeds Of Time

The seeds of time,
Are etched upon,
Your skin so gracefully,
The memories,
Of years gone by,
Are all that's left for me.

Aimlessly,
I search for what,
I did not find in you,
But do I seek,
For what I want,
Is what I'm after true.

My heart is cold,
My soul is dry,
I do not wish to be,
A lonely man,
Who cannot find,
The fruit upon the tree.

The wrinkled skin,
Upon my face,
It sadly hides my age,
The voice within,
That nags at me,
It fills my heart with rage.

Did I give up,
Too easily,
The lose was much to great,
Please return,
My soul to me,
It's still at heaven's gate,

If returned,
A better man,
I'll surely try to be,
To waste a chance,
That's given twice,
Could never set me free.

I do not wish,
To die alone,
And so I give to you,
My love within,
Forevermore,
Yes this I wish to do.

The Voice

The wisdom of the voice I hear,
Forever full of sin,
Keeps me on the narrow path,
It seems I cannot win.

The race is on, the bullet fired,
Where do I go from here,
The eyes that watch me from within,
Always reappear.

I wish to go with you my love,
Please change the path I'm on,
To help me find the safest route,
Surely can't be wrong.

The voice is loud, too loud for me,
It forever drowns my mind,
With things I cannot comprehend,
If only I could find.

A love to conquer all my fears,
To drown the voice within,
My search is long, but soon shall end,
I'll be with you again.

The Winter Frost Shall Weep

Four travelers so young,
Passed upon a world of white,
Is this perhaps the place their looking for, Four strangers in a foreign land,
Living beyond their dreams,
The time has come to find the hidden door.

Within the night so cold,
Is when the bitter tears shall flow.
The Ice Queen glares through shallow,
sunken eyes,
The winter stays forever,
And never will seasons change,
Until the time when hearts so cold shall die.

If compassion can't be found,
Within-the confines of your life,
Then dream my friend, allow yourself to sleep,
The lesson lived is the lesson learned.
The love shall melt the heart,
And soon enough the winter frost shall weep.

The Word Within

An Angel whispered to me in,
The quiet of the night,
I fear for what she has to say,
For something isn't right.

She touches me with worried words,
For someone that I know,
Who's pain is more than she can bear,
Or should ever .have to know.

I know not what I can offer you,
To help you ease your pain,
Other than a single word,
That will give you strength again.

The word, it may be small in size,
And yet it means so much,
For me to offer it to you,
For you to carress its touch.

To cast away the pain you feel,
As only true friends can do,
Look within yourself and fight,
Your heart will lead you true.

The word I offer you is HOPE,
Embrace it strong and win,
For it comes from those who care the most,
And whose hearts you'll always be in.

These Simple Joys

I scatter pebbles upon the beach,
To pass the hours away,
I love them best, these simple joys,
That get me through my days.

I lay upon the grass so green,
And stare into the sky,
Just to find a face within,
The clouds which float so high.

I walk through fields of lavender,
Just because I can,
My reasons are my own to know,
That I am who I am.

A better person takes the time,
To seek what can be found,
I love them best, these simple joys,
They're simply all around.

These Thoughts Within

Your shimmering locks of golden hair,
They radiate a light,
That ignites a fire in your eyes,
And warms my heart tonight.

The touch of gentle fingertips,
Upon my skin is soft,
Your whispers kiss my inner thoughts,
And send my cares aloft.

The ruby red of pulsing lips,
My senses can't deny,
Your step ignites my weary eyes,
They cannot tell a lie.

My heart it pounds a steady beat,
Whenever you are near,
My pulse increases when your voice,
Is nibbling on my ear.

If two can share these thoughts within,
Then everything is right,
I give my all for you alone,
And you alone tonight.

Three Simple Words

Upon the mantle, Atop the hearth,
Sits a lonely soul,
A picture of,
The one I loved,
So many years ago.

My memories,
Are evidence,
Of feelings I denied,
And so the trust,
I should have shown,
Was trapped within the lies.

My love for her,
Was always strong,
And yet I could not say,
Three simple words,
Within my heart,
Until her dying day.

Now she sits,
Atop the hearth,
I never question why,
Within my heart,
She shall remain,
Until the day I die.

To Me You Were The Best

I know that time,
Cannot erase,
My memories of you,
A friend you always,
Were to me,
Your heart was always true.

And as we grew,
Throughout the years,
We changed in many ways,
But in our minds,
We formed a bond,
That was never led astray.

And so the years,
They slowly passed,
As years so often do,
And even though,
We were far apart,
I often thought of you.

Now fate did strike,
A viscious blow,
And all that's left for me,
Are precious thoughts,
And precious dreams,
And precious memories.

A better place,
I know you're in,
And so my heart can rest,
For you will always,
Be my friend,
To me you were the best.

Too High A Price

Wanton thoughts that rage behind,
The never-closing doors,
Ignite the fires that burn within,
The tales of lust and lore.

The sacrificial rite is made,
The lamb upon the stone,
Those who wield the blood-stained knife, Shall forever be alone.

Sinking down to darkened depths,
The heart is black as coal,
Their greed is darkness from within,
Rotten is the soul.

Too high a price when lives are lost,
And never shall they see,
The vile stench that seeps through pores,
Of those so full of greed.

The ones who sacrifice their hearts,
Will only lose in the end,
For what goes around, comes around,
Again and again and again.

To Write Is Love

I've often felt,
That perhaps if,
I give a little more,
The kindness given,
Might return,
Come flowing through my door.

My ink and paper,
Serve a need,
That only seems to keep,
My heart from slowly,
Sinking down,
To levels much to deep.

Life is full,
Of so much strife,
Sometimes I feel a need,
To,give it up,
Just walk away,
My heart could surely bleed.

I do not want,
To sacrifice,
My inner self for you,
It's not for me,
To do for you,
What I would never do.

So write I do,
And write I will,
Yes I am what it's for,
I'll never tire,
To write is love,
To me forevermore.

True Hearts Sit Side By Side

To test the feelings,
Of the one,
Who's heart won't be denied,
Could only serve,
To sever dreams,
Wherein our thoughts do hide.

My mind you haunt,
Through night and day,
Yet no fear have I felt,
The cards are on,
The table now,
I know not what I've dealt.

The sun doth filter,
Through thy locks,
Of softly flowing hair,
The grace and beauty,
Upon your face,
Could trap me unawares.

There's so much pain,
Within your eyes,
They cannot lie to me,
You seek for what,
Your heart needs most,
So why must your heart always bleed.

I wish to see,
You smile again,
The beauty held within,
Will flow through you,
Forevermore,
Your heart will always win.

I know of how,
You feel inside,
Yes, I've walked through that door,
To lose in love,
Is a bitter pill,
I wish to swallow no more.

Your heart will never,
Lie to you,
True love can't be denied,
My friend you are,
Forevermore,
True hearts sit side by side.

Two Wishes Left For Me

He rides on clouds of milky white,
Forever wandering free,
Alone he soars through darkened skies,
A lonely man is he.

He thinks about a woman he met,
A vision for all to see,
Will he see her once again,
A lonely man is he.

Three wishes from the magic lamp,
Is all he really needs,
The first fulfilled, the others not,
A lonely man is he.

She drowns his mind with thoughts unsure,
Does she feel the need,
To be with one who's heart is lost,
A lonely man is he.

They'll meet again, or so he hopes,
Two wishes left to see,
But will she open up her heart,
A lonely man is he,
Two wishes left for me.

Visions Of Tomorrow

Rush to the door,
Don't run outside,
Break the silence,
Of the fears we hide.

Forever lost,
Within our minds,
Break out and be free,
Let go the binds.

Never comes the day,
When all are free,
Blessed are the hearts,
Of the ones who see.

Travel distant roads,
That have no end in sight,
Don't give in to madness,
Never give up the fight.

See Beyond your limits.
Look for what's not there,
See visions of tomorrow,
The signs are everywhere.

Walls

I pacify my memories,
With thoughts I cannot share,
The loss is mine and mine alone,
And still my heart can care.

My life is locked within my past,
A wall that no one sees,
A door whose only key is love,
And love is what I need.

Many times I've tried to break,
A hole within these walls,
The only hammer strong enough,
Has never walked these halls.

And so I wait for what I know,
Alone I'll never see,
The beauty of the strength of love,
That burns inside of me.

If your heart can crush these walls,
And show me that you care,
Then I can give forevermore,
What I have never dared.

Wishes

Your laughter sparks the heart within,
The souls of those you touch,
Your heart requires more than this,
For this is not enough,
To satisfy your inner needs,
You set your mind at will,
Your loneliness is wishes made,
But never quite fulfilled.

Your path is traveled long and hard,
Your shoes have worn their soles,
And are you any closer now,
To reaching all your goals,
Take the hand that reaches forth,
To guide you once again,
Time is better traveled,
When two friends can share their pain.

I sense in you a need to find,
What's lost within your life,
Your heart has many questions strong,
The answer's never right,
The funny thing with wishes though.
Is soon enough you'll see,
That wishes born of loving hearts,
Are always within reach.

Within

The pedestal you sit upon,
Shall be your only throne,
Your kingdom reaches far and wide,
Within the confines of your home.

The thoughts you ponder slowly,
Are never left too far behind,
You share your dreams with one and all,
Within the confines of your mind.

You wish that you were young again,
Yet age must take it's toll,
And so your youth is buried deep,
Within the confines of your soul.

You wish that you could love again,
And make a fresh new start,
But love for you is just a word,
Within the confines of your heart.

So look beyond what you percieve,
And perhaps you will find,
That everything you need is here,
Within the confines of my mind.

Within My Heart

I tuck you in,
And kiss your cheek,
As gently as a dove,
The joy I feel,
Within my heart,
Surrounds me like a glove.

I hold your tiny,
Hands in mine,
So soft and yet so strong,
Hy love for you,
Will never fade,
And this can never be wrong.

So peaceful is,
The innocence,
I see upon your face,
These memories,
Are solid gold,
And cannot be erased.

I hope that life,
Will treat you well,
And keep you from harms way,
I'll do my best,
To understand,
If ever you should stray.

And though I know,
The time will come,
When I must let you go,
Within my heart,
My daughters love,
Will forever show.

Words

BITTER is the man who seeks,
What he knows he'll never find,
LONELY is the man who leaves,
Compassion far behind.

CARING is the man who gives,
To those he never knows,
LOVING is the man to whom,
The children always go.

NARROW is the man who cannot,
See beyond his reach,
SHALLOW is the man who feels,
There's nothing left to teach.

GRACIOUS is the man who shares,
The little things in life,
PRECIOUS is the man who lives,
For what he knows is right.

ANGRY is the man who cannot,
Live with who he is,
IGNORANT is the man who thinks,
He has nothing to give.

HUMBLE is the man who can,
Admit to all his fears,
PATIENT is the man who always,
Lends a willing ear.

SADDENED is the man who feels,
He's nothing left to gain,
SHAMEFUL is the man who feels,
That he's always to blame.

CONTENT is the man who's never,
Forever asking why,
JOYFUL is the man who hears,
A newborn baby cry.

All these WORDS, I give to you,
For all eternity,
Share them with a friend or two,
Perhaps, they're just like me.

You Decorate

You decorate,
Your lonely halls,
With things you do not need,
Pictures cover,
Broken walls,
That only make you bleed.

You decorate,
Your lonely heart,
With wounds that never heal,
You tried to buy,
Your happiness,
With things you could not steal.

You decorate,
Your lonely soul,
With things you know are wrong,
And so you lose,
The freedom found,
In keeping one's self strong.

You decorate,
Your lonely life,
With things that make you hate,
The voice that beckons,
In the night,
Now tells you it's too late.

I'll decorate,
Your lonely grave,
With thoughts you never shared,
For I alone,
Knew all along,
That you really cared.

You'll Hurt Me Nevermore

Unforbidden, unrestricted,
Love is all I ask,
Your soul ignites my beating heart,
Flashing memories repast.

Sunshine is the light of day,
Darkness is the moon,
I haven't been here for awhile,
Perhaps I'll return soon.

Hearts can snap like breaking glass,
All scattered upon the floor,
Mine is made of solid steel,
You'll hurt me nevermore.

Your passion is the spark.
That lights my ever-raging fires,
To dream of things of eons past,
Shall spark long lost desires.

But if the wine is tainted,
And the blood flows from your pores.
Remember, solid is my heart,
You'll hurt me nevermore.

You Will Always Hold My Heart

The time that I have spent with you,
I'll treasure all my years,
The beauty of your charm and grace,
Will always calm my fears.

I wish that I could find a way,
To gently let you know,
That even though I wish to stay,
I know that I must go.

The words I need to hear from you,
Alone could make me stay,
I know your heart has seen its pain,
But please don't make mine pay.

For I can look within myself,
And know my heart can rest,
You are all I need in life,
To me you are the best.

Now I will go if go I must,
I'd rather be with you,
For you will always hold my heart,
No matter what you choose.

Your Ball And Chain

A candle sits atop the hearth,
It casts an eerie glow,
The shadows upon the wall are those,
Which have nowhere to go,
You sit and ponder what it was,
That wouldn't let you go.

You tiptoe past the silent one,
Who holds your ball and chain,
You have no strength to find the door,
And so you lose again,
Your hopes are slowly chipped away,
And so your heart knows pain.

You sit and ponder what it was,
Your mind forgot to show,
How could life have trapped you here,
So many years ago,
You try to find a memory,
That no one else could know.

Now you alone can free your soul,
From what should never be,
I wish that you could look within,
And tell me what you see,
Your ball and chain is in your heart,
There both attached to me.

Your Gift Within

I look upon,
The playful smile,
That adds a touch of grace,
To the beauty,
And subtle charm,
I see upon your face.

I look into,
Your fiery eyes,
And recognize the fears,
That haunt our hearts,
And daunt our souls,
Throughout the living years.

I look around,
And see the souls,
Of those your heart has touched,
Your kindness gives,
Through how you live,
And that can do so much.

I look upon,
The playful smile,
That gently teases my heart,
Your gift within, Is given free,
A place for all to start.

Your Heart Is Everywhere

I cast a glance,
Across the room,
To see what it is I hear,
A voice like Angels,
Whispers soft,
And gently kisses my ear.

Her flowing locks,
Of shimmering gold,
Fall softly upon her face,
Her smile warms,
The coldest night,
And sets my heart to race.

A fire burns,
Within her eyes,
And plants a single seed,
And when her heart,
Ignites with flame,
Her passions shall be freed.

For that which burns,
Within her soul,
Is kindness, joy and care,
For I have looked,
Beyond and know,
Your heart is everywhere.

Your Heart Lives All Alone

The simple joys within our lives,
Are those we get for free,
Always there for everyone,
But not for you and me.

I sense a loss within your heart,
You did not find desire,   _
The search was such a waste of time,
My heartlight sparks yoUR fires.

My passion flows within your pores,
And yet I cannot touch,
A entle kiss upon your lips,
Might satisfy my lust.

The broken hearts and battered souls,
We live with day to day,
Are lost within a system which,
Knows compassion strayed.

Your heart lives all alone my friend,
And nothing can I do,
I wish my reach was stronger,
For I cannot watch you lose.

I

Your Heart Will Always Care

Many times I've wished to quench,
The thirst that drives your pain,
The passageway is buried deep,
The heartache still remains.

Your mask is growing thinner,
As you ponder through your days,
To remove it much too quickly,
Blurs your mind and their you'll stay.

Yet you have never given in,
And though the fight is hard,
For every inch you lose to waste,
Your strength gives back a yard.

I love you in a special way,
As only true friends can share,
For you are worth my time and I know,
Your heart will always care.

Your Key Is Love

The heart which gives,
A little more,
Will always find the key,
To unlock doors,
Of sheltered hearts,
And set their passions free.

The two of you,
Have formed a bond,
That no one can forsake,
For love can conquer,
Many fears,
And open many gates.

Your destiny,
Is yours to choose,
You both have hosen wise,
Your love grows stronger,
Every day,
It's written in your eyes.

Your key is love,
Forevermore,
And in your hearts you will know,
That what you give,
Was always there,
And that will always show.

Your Own Reality

The lonely story of your life,
Is whispered through your walls,
The fingerprints of years gone by,
Decorate your halls.

Secrets better left untold,
Hiding beneath the stairs,
Waiting oh so patiently,
To trap you unawares.

Faces fading in the night,
Of those you see each day,
Your memory wonserve you here,
For your attention strayed.

Diversions dull your useless thoughts,
And yet it always seems,
You get more satisfaction,
From your life within your dreams.

Time to wake and look around,
Tell me what you see,
the dream is over; it's time to live,
Your own reality.

About the Author

The majority of these poems were written while he was a member of the Canadian Navy. He would sit out on the upper deck at night and look at the stars, and this is where most of his inspiration came from. Sometimes family and friends, mostly women, would ask him to write a poem for them, and that is where some of them also came from.

Made in the USA
Middletown, DE
27 January 2018